The Intimacy Superpower

7 Ways to be Unstoppable in Life and Love
Updated Edition

Jai Simone

Catalyst Life Global
♡

Dedication

To all who wanted my "secret sauce," thank you for your support!!!
To everyone who encouraged my curiosity... to the brave souls who traveled these paths with me... to the lifestyle folks who welcomed me ... I appreciate you!

To my Lock, thank you for the inspiration!

Contents

Introduction

This is a book about sex, right?

Are you looking to connect with your partner in new and exciting ways? Maybe just reconnect? Increase your happiness? Perhaps simply find a partner for connection? Become your best self? After working with singles. couples, CEOs, teachers, military, zero figure incomes, 7 figure incomes, entrepreneurs, men, women, non-binary, cis, queer, monogamous, poly, and the multitudes in between, it has become clear to me that intimacy in one form or another was needed to resolve their issues. Most people think of intimacy as sex or what happens to make people sexual. They are not wrong. They are just not entirely right.

Intimacy is what people crave when they are alone at night. It has helped completely change the course of my clients' lives. Intimacy is what helps someone in depression choose not to take their own life. Intimacy is what bonds spouses who thought divorce was the only answer. Intimacy is what prompted some of my clients to change jobs and receive substantially higher pay. Intimacy is what helped the manager become a better boss and their staff more productive. Intimacy is what propelled that single who desperately desired to be in a relationship finally find joy in life and a partner who added to that pleasure. Intimacy is what helped the artist break open new doors and it is what helps clients shake off their fear and follow their dreams. Intimacy is not just one thing.

Intimate is defined as a warm friendship; sex or sexual relations; a personal or private nature; and **intrinsic, essential; belonging to or characterizing one's deepest nature.** Though we will be exploring many aspects of intimacy, this last definition is critical. It is the closeness of things, so essential in all close relationships. Just as a restaurant can be intimate, so too can you be intimate with yourself or someone else. As we explore each Intimacy, you will see certain things are intrinsic, meaning they belongs there. Just as you belong here, learning more about the very thing that will elevate your life. As you get closer to yourself, friends, partner(s), you might learn that you each have different intimacy styles. What types of intimacy are most important to you? To them? Use the suggestions from those sections to connect more fully. Things are about to get very interesting!

There have been discussions among academics, therapists and coaches for decades regarding how many types of intimacy exist. Here we will explore the seven most recognized, Emotional, Intellectual, Experiential, Creative, Spiritual, Conflict, and Physical. If you can delve into and implement these seven fully, I guarantee that your life will change. Your current relationships and future interactions will drastically improve. You will indeed be able to wield the Intimacy Superpower. Let us take this journey to discover how to capitalize on each intimacy in Life and Love.

Where it All Began...

HOW TO CONNECT WITH OTHERS

There are people whose very lives are devoted to connecting with people instantly, from con artists to customer service reps, spies to motivational speakers, undercover agents to high priced escorts. What do they know that you do not?

Maslow's Hierarchy of Needs

Let us start with the basics. According to Maslow's Hierarchy of Needs, every person needs five things to be satisfied with their lives:

Physiological, Safety, Belongingness and Love, Esteem, and Self-actualization. (illustration) Though this theory originally states that one must travel through each level to even desire the next (starting from the bottom), we have found that this pyramid may rearrange itself at different phases of life for certain people; but the fact remains that we all must have these in some capacity. Each level can be intertwined with another as well. Some view safety through the lens of relationships. The same with Esteem. Think about infants. Their Physiological needs, Safety, Love, Esteem all come from their proximity to another. As we develop, we often gain the capacity to provide the Physiological needs for ourselves, though food and drink can often be more enjoyable when sharing.

Let us imagine a zombie apocalypse, which happens to be one of my favorite pastimes. You may have a thousand guns, plenty of ammo, a cellar full of food, a reservoir worth of water and still feel unsafe. In this situation, it is better to have a number greater than one. Who will shoot your other guns, take a shift while you sleep, etc? While true intimacy begins with you, sharing it with others is what makes it magic. We will discuss ways to gain what is needed for you to become the kind of person who has The Intimacy Superpower, but right now, let us begin at the beginning, initial connection.

If you do not have an issue meeting people, you may want to skip to the next chapter.

How Do I Meet People?

Whether you born an introvert, extrovert, ambivert/ omnivert, the majority of humans are social creatures. It has been hardwired into us since our earliest ancestors worked together to endure. Humans have evolved to see faces in everyday objects, facial pareidolia, because being able to distinguish emotions helps you survive. This is why smiling is such a powerful act. Not all humans have the pareidolia ability, but if you do, it helps you establish social cues from others. I have had clients ask me why no one ever approaches them when they go out. They have tried dressing up, using makeup, making eye contact, but nothing works. I then asked them if they smiled at all during this time period and they could not remember doing so. Looking friendly has a way of helping you make friends. Looking sullen is a defense mechanism used by many people. It does not mean they are unapproachable (though sometimes this is EXACTLY what it means), it simply means their resting face is serious. (Side note: Do not demand that a woman smile. It is not her job to perform for you.)

Taking the first step can be terrifying. Right now, you just need to feel confident enough to walk up to someone and begin a conversation. If you have anxiety, this will seem like a monumental task. Just know that your anxiety is normal. I have faith in you. It is easier to speak to someone in a more agreeable venue, a bookstore, a Con, a class, whatever locale makes you feel more capable/ knowledgeable/comfortable. Where is your happy place? Go there. You already have something in common because you are both at the same location. Gather your courage and give an honest compliment. Not everyone is going to respond the way you would like, but this is a numbers game. The more you do it, the better you become. The better you become, the more likely it is that you receive the response you desire. Many of my clients with social anxiety have had success with this daunting first step, so it truly is possible. I believe in you!

Now that you have crossed that hurdle, let's make you a better conversationalist. What makes people tick? People LOVE to talk about themselves and/or things they perceive as theirs, children/grandchildren, research, pets, obsessions, collections, creative pursuits, niche knowledge, etc. They love feeling like they are special, while simultaneously fitting in. Simply ask them about themselves in an interesting way. You can do it! An initial greeting can look something like this: " I love your anklet, hair pin, character on phone case, industrial piercing jewelry, picture of their children/grandchildren, sticker on their laptop, etc." The point of this is to mention something small that everyone may not notice. You can always complement shoes, but I would like you to dig a little deeper. Does their shirt have a saying from a cult classic? Comment on that! You should then follow up with a question that shows you are interested in said thing. What is their favorite character from that show? Does that hair pin symbolize their birthstone? Do you also read banned books? (I have an "I read banned books" sticker on my laptop.) After the initial greeting, you can introduce yourself. Then expand on what you were discussing. Focus on them.

There are many different means one can use to connect with another. Here are three powerful techniques.

Ask questions. Remember, people enjoy talking about themselves. Ask them questions about their interests. Ask if they have any pets or are working on anything that excites them.

Active Listening. As they are talking, do not simply sit awaiting your turn to speak. Listen closely so you can ask follow up questions. What are they saying in addition to the speech? Do they convey excitement, sadness, fear, joy…? Try to listen beyond just the words. This lets the other person know they are being heard. Active listening is crucial to all of the intimacies, so mastering it early is a huge bonus!

Thirdly, **mirroring.** Now that you have been actively listening, you can mirror their tone and pace. You can also sprinkle in key words or phrases they have used. This builds rapport very quickly. If you can get someone to talk to you, you can build a relationship!

As they say, "Teamwork makes the dream work." Humans are built for teams, be it of 2, 5, 22 or 1000. This closeness between people and ourselves, this feeling of safety with another helps us slowly learn to trust. This is the foundation upon which all others are built.

Just so you know, people are really rooting for you. Think of all of the people on dating apps, joining online groups for friendships, those who are simply wishing for company. Everyone is

hoping the next person they meet is "The One."
You may be exactly who they are looking for, but
first you have to meet! You have the power to
change both of your lives.

Let's Begin!

Increased intimacy is not just for romantic relationships. It can significantly improve platonic, familial, and professional relationships as well. Learning and implementing tips from this section will allow you to grow as a person. I have had many clients who focus on one form of intimacy at a time to evolve into a more enlightened and satisfied version of themselves, someone capable of mature interpersonal relationships. Look at you, already on your way to winning at life!

Self-intimacy allows you trust yourself more, find it easier to empathize with others, and properly communicate your wants and needs. When you understand your desires, you can work together to create a shared set of rules in your relationships. Creating and enforcing healthy boundaries is critical to your work/play/happiness balance. Working on yourself allows this to become your new normal. You are able to maintain necessary boundaries with love, while also building stronger bonds with others. Whether used in a romantic relationship, platonic one, or yourself, implementing the intimacies allows you to know people from the inside, much deeper than anyone else. Let's go become our best selves!

Before beginning this journey through the **Emotional, Intellectual, Experiential, Creative, Spiritual, Conflict,** and **Physical Intimacies,** I would like you to take a few minutes of alone time and just sit with yourself. ...

...How does it feel? What do you hear? Are you lonely, relaxed, enlightened, uncomfortable? How long can you maintain the silence? There are no right or wrong answers. Wherever you are is where you are. There is no judgement here. I just want you to make a note of it.

Emotional

It has been said that adulthood is simply overcoming the trauma of childhood. While we know that is not all adulthood is about, it does hold some truth. Emotional baggage keeps us from being the freest form of ourselves. We are shackled to a past situation, person or feeling. This prevents us from being fully present in some situations and living the life we truly desire. Sometimes it keeps us alone, other times it keeps us surrounded with people unable to hear our own voice.

Just my opinion, but everyone should see a therapist at some point. You may not feel like you have a heavy trauma to tackle or did not have enough happen to you to warrant seeing someone, but I beg to differ. Everyone has something in their lives that could benefit from being brought into the light. Sometimes it could be something as simple as sharing a secret that has been too heavy to hold in. It does not have to be yours. It could be that talking about your job allows

22

you to see that you really should move on to another company. Possibly discussing your past can unlock answers you could not see on your own. Talking about it with an objective professional can offer profound breakthroughs. Try it and see.

Emotional self intimacy also involves being kind to yourself. We spend 100% of our time with ourselves. It is the longest relationship we will ever have, but for some, it is not very loving. For this, I suggest building affirmations into your morning and/or evening routine. Look at yourself in the mirror and tell yourself you are amazing. You are! So far, you have a 100% success rate against those things designed to destroy you. Please give yourself the credit you deserve!

***

Have you ever met someone and just felt immediately connected to them? The kind of person who makes you feel comfortable being yourself or that you are somehow friends after a short time? They are the kind of person who radiates warmth. This is Emotional Intimacy at work. Emotional Intimacy involves a perception of closeness to another, sharing of personal feelings, and personal validation.

Do you know the sayings, "you need money to make money" or "you have to give to get" or "it takes one to know one"? Well, these things are mostly true. To receive Emotional Intimacy, you must also know how to give Emotional Intimacy. You must understand that trust, listening and non-judgement are cornerstones. You have it in you! There is a positive, powerful energy that exists between people who feel heard, seen, valued.

An Emotion Wheel, originally created by Robert Plutchik, is helpful to accurately describe what you are feeling. Accuracy in emotions helps you identify what either you or your friend/partner may be feeling. It is very useful in determining how to properly respond to your/their needs. Each emotion in the Wheel serves an evolutionary function and can trigger survival behaviors. In modern society, some of these behaviors may take the form of running away from people or situations due to fear or self-sabotage, not trusting in relationships, or panic attacks. Using the Wheel can help as a visual aid for converting negative emotions to positive ones.

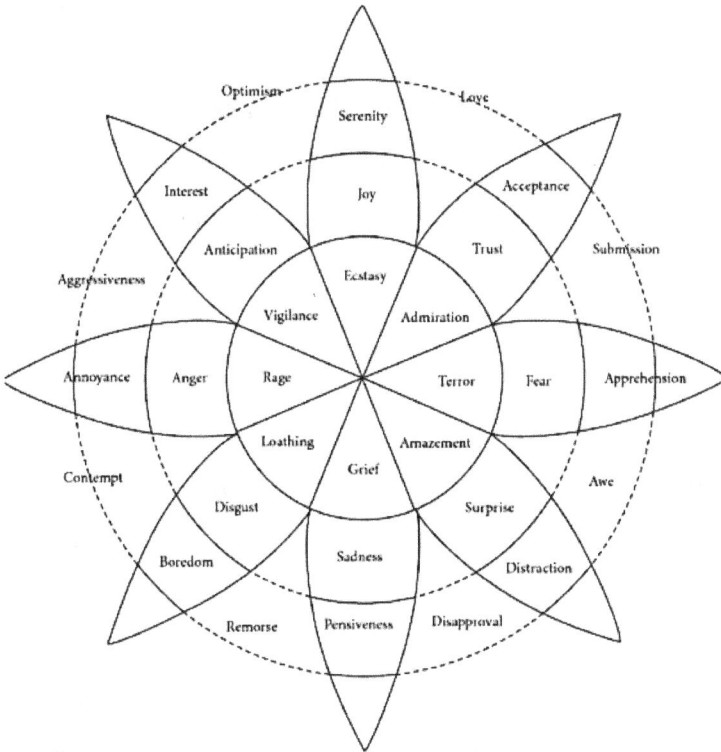

Emotion Wheel
The emotions in the center, in clockwork order, are ecstasy, admiration, terror, amazement, grief, loathing, rage, and vigilance.

The words at the center are the deepest versions of the core emotions illustrated on Plutchik's original Wheel. He said the core emotions are joy, trust, fear, surprise, sadness, disgust, anger and anticipation. You will notice that they are the level after the center. You can then move outward to identify additional emotions. The words outside of the circle are combinations of the closest emotions illustrated. Some actions or reactions to feelings are out of our control, but others, like responses to fear or anger, are not. Mastering Emotional Intimacy requires mastering and sharing your emotions. The Emotion Wheel is a great tool to begin that process.

Due to past fear, trauma or upbringing, some find emotional intimacy to be terrifying. If you believe that you can no longer share your heart with someone and that is the hill you are going to die on, PLEASE let a therapist help you find a path down from that lonely peak.

Intellectual

"Sharp-tongued writer Mark Twain and electricity wizard Nikola Tesla forged a famous friendship around their shared intellectual curiosity. The two titans of the Gilded Age often exchanged letters after meeting in the New York social scene of the 1890s, and Twain was a frequent visitor to Tesla's lab. During many hours in this workshop of scientific oddities, Tesla wowed the novelist with demonstrations of high voltage electricity, and the men also experimented with early x-ray photography.

So great was Tesla and Twain's mutual admiration that each man even claimed the other had once cured him of an illness. In his autobiography, Tesla wrote that when he was bedridden from sickness as a young man, Twain's "captivating" novels had been a much-needed solace that helped jump-start a recovery. After the two became friends, Tesla repaid the favor when he cured the writer of a severe bout of constipation by having him stand on a high frequency oscillator." (history.com)

Indulging in a single intimacy can build lifelong friendships, as evidenced by Twain and Tesla. Like them, learning something new everyday has been a goal of mine since childhood. I have always been curious and devoted to reading everything I could. Intellectual pursuits keep your mind sharp and help you become more interesting. You become great at dinner parties, networking events and will perhaps be added to someone's Phone A Friend list! Besides making you a deipnosophist (master dinner conversationalist. Look at you learning new things already!), intellectual self intimacy also allows you to enjoy the inner workings of your own mind. Your mind has new places to wander. You will find that you actually enjoy your own company. You are smart and capable already, but pursuing an intellectual bond with yourself makes you even more so.

***

Whether you took first place at every science fair or had no idea that the World's Fair was for inventions and the achievements of nations, you can engage in Intellectual Intimacy. It is more about accepting the inner workings of your mind without judgement than anything else.

Ways to cultivate Intellectual Intimacy with yourself

1. Read! Try books that challenge your ideas and perspective. It will force you to reevaluate your previous notions and decide where you stand.

2. Write poetry. It does not have to be submitted for a Poet Laureate position, but it will allow you to express yourself in new ways.

3. Try "The Raisin Exercise" a mindfulness experience. First choose a food, ideally small, with an interesting texture, smell and/or taste. Pay close attention to several things:

   - How does it look
   - How does it feel?
   - How does it make your skin feel when touching/holding/manipulating it?
   - How does it smell?
   - How does it taste?

Paying attention and being aware of ourselves and environment is becoming increasingly rare. Bring yourself into the moment and notice things within yourself. Try this whenever you feel your mind becoming too cluttered and chaotic.

Experiential

A few years ago "dating yourself" was a popular phrase. The concept is wonderful! Sometimes we can get so involved with others and life happening that we don't even remember what we like to do. This is especially true if you have a partner and/or children. You are so busy doing what they need and want that you may fall to the back burner. Doing things, whatever those things may be, builds confidence and memories. Relationships survive harsh times with memories and the hope of building new ones.

So I want you to make a list of things you enjoy, enjoyed or think you might want to enjoy and then … wait for it … go do them! It is better than waiting on others and never getting to do those things. Wouldn't you rather experience life than just hear about others having grand adventures? I am not saying it has to be a grand adventure, simply your adventure. Do you like reading? Join a book club. Movies? Take yourself to a matinee. No one ever said you can't be a cheap date! Do you like comic books, go to Comic Con and make some new friends! There is a club for everything these days. You can also find a virtual tribe. Online groups for pretty much every activity under the sun have been created. Go join one! That being said, you should absolutely take yourself to a museum or conference on crocheting or ballroom dancing class or hobby shop to learn to play Magic the Gathering. Whatever your interest may be, pursue it! You will find you are much happier with your life.

This may seem scary at first, but after you have done things by yourself a few times, I promise it will be easier. Plus, that satisfied feeling will remain much longer than your nervous energy. You can do it!

***

Forrest Gump may live simply, but his life was proof that Experiential Intimacy can form lifelong bonds. He and Bubba experienced so much together that they became fast friends. Forrest's experiences with Lt Dan connected them for life.

There are many reasons why people remain friends, but when you get together there is inevitably a discussion that begins, "Do you remember that time we…" The memories shared are the glue that hold many friendships together. This is Experiential Intimacy. You have common ground, similar points of reference, the ability to add to the conversation and a foundation to build additional memories. Usually these are happy memories, so you also are associated with a positive moment in the other's life. Keep doing these things! You are part of the reason they smile. That is powerful indeed.

Creative

They say painting is calming. My artistic ability is limited to stick figures, but creative pursuits are great for building different types of connections in your brain. Plus, you can have something to hang on your wall! Obviously the creative is not limited to drawing, painting, sculpting - it is anything you can imagine! Through writing I can create entire worlds. If you can sew, anything you make is a new creation. I've seen people make houses out of legos, cities out of matchsticks, cars out yarn. You can simply go to a paint & sip, go to a cake decorating class or write a haiku. The goal is not to create a masterpiece on your first try, but to expand your concept of you. Try a new hobby, impress yourself and get those creative juices flowing!

"Everyone falls into creative ruts, but two people rarely do so at the same time." -James Somers

There are many creatives who collaborate and find they construct something larger than themselves after doing so. Creative intimacy has the power to outlast both of you. This bond can be legendary!

***

Herakut is the fusion of Aka Hera and Falk Akut Lehmann, a German street artist duo who met in 2004 during an international graffiti festival. Hera brings to the duo academic training and Akut, a skill for spray-paint acquired in the street. She draws and does the sketches, while he fills up, and adds details and realism. Their unique murals, which include sweet animals wearing hats and objects in awkward positions, can be found in big cities around the world.

Spiritual

Mindfulness is all the rage right now. Being present is incredibly important to your satisfaction in life. Being centered is what you want to strive for. This can happen through various means; meditation, yoga, prayer, chakra alignment. There is no religious affiliation with spiritual self intimacy, merely an opportunity to get to know the real you. What are your beliefs about the world, the spiritual realm, your relation to it? How do these translate to how you treat yourself and others? Can you feel the "god" in you, however that may manifest? Through simple silence and questioning, you can expand your awareness of yourself. An added benefit is the outside world will not effect you nearly as much.

Many people find their closest friends are those they find in church, temple, mosque, Wiccan meetup, American Atheists National Convention, etc. There is something about being accepted for something you believe with the very core of your being that makes fast friends. In these situations, it is absolutely acceptable to talk religion!

***

In the early 1920s, master escape artist Harry Houdini and "Sherlock Holmes" author Sir Arthur Conan Doyle struck up an offbeat friendship. Houdini was a natural skeptic, fond of debunking psychics and supposed paranormal phenomena, while Conan Doyle was a born believer who served as an evangelist for the Spiritualist movement. Nevertheless, the two frequently traded letters and books, and once even vacationed together.

Desperate to make his friend believe in the power of psychic mediums, Conan Doyle took to dragging Houdini to different séances around Europe. But with each flawed reading, Houdini became even more convinced the practice was the work of frauds and hucksters. The relationship finally reached its breaking point in 1923, after

Conan Doyle and his wife organized a disastrous séance where they tried to contact Houdini's deceased mother in the afterlife. After trading insults in warring New York Times columns, the two stopped speaking altogether.(history.com) And in other situations, it is best to not discuss religion. In this instance (as in most), one party would not allow the other to be themselves. They did not honor their freedom. With any intimacy, we are here to accept our friend/partner. They do not have to agree or be carbon copies of us. This was not a safe space.

Conflict

As mentioned with Emotional Intimacy, we all carry baggage. Most of us also have a little voice inside telling us we are not worthy or enough. This is such a difficult intimacy to confront, but worth all of the effort. By resolving some of the conflicts with our inner negative voice and the bright future we envision for ourselves, we begin a path towards our highest selves. To do this, try journaling or take a seminar on shadow work. Affirmations done in conjunction with power poses can help you focus on your goal of positive speaking to yourself. Count your successes daily. Begin a personal resume listing all of the obstacles you have overcome, positive things you've done, and/or lives positively changed because of you. If you can see how accomplished you are, even if just tiny acts, you will understand that you are indeed worthy and more than enough. I believe in you!

Conquering Conflict

According to the Gottman Institute, there are a few conflicts styles, aptly nicknamed The Four Horseman. The Four Horseman in literature are often believed to symbolize the end of the world/ apocalypse and consistently using these elements will bring about the end of any relationship.

The Four Horseman of Conflict are:

- Criticism - Verbally attacking personality or character
- Contempt - Attacking sense of self with intent to insult or abuse.
- Defensiveness - victimizing yourself to ward off perceived attack and reverse the blame.
- Stonewalling - Withdrawing to avoid conflict, conveying disapproval, distance, and separation.

Most likely you have been the recipient of each of these tactics. Perhaps you have also been the harbinger of each as well. Conflict is natural, even within yourself, so we are not trying to eliminate it. We are simply trying to do all we can to realize the functional, positive aspects of conflict that provide opportunities for growth and understanding. Be gentle with yourself during this stage, but also work to manage the negative aspects of your conflict communication to effectively connect with yourself and others.

Here are some suggestions regarding the moment conflict arises.

- Be silent if you cannot say it without screaming.
- Be silent when you are feeling critical.
- Be silent in the heat of anger.
- Be silent when you do not have all of the facts.
- Breathe. Breathe. Breathe. Then speak

Remember that love can be nurturing and soft, but it is also tough and revealing. It will show you the sides of yourself that need work. Allow love to be all of its forms.

When you are at conflict with yourself or another, try to ask yourself what the real problem may be. What is really being said? Does it have any basis in your reality? Use this information to formulate your solution. If the conflict is in your head, try one or all of the following. Recall situations where you were successful - be it a spelling bee, foot race, video game, or simply getting out of bed when you did not think you had the physical or emotional strength to do so. Being reminded of winning, no matter how small you may have convinced yourself it was, can help combat negative talk. Your wins need to be celebrated in these moments. I am proud of you!

Sometimes merely doing another action is enough to eliminate the issue. If you hear your voice of conflict harping on the activity you are doing at the moment, change it. Distract yourself. The mind generally does not hold both of those things at once. You can do affirmations at this point, but why not think of things that bring you joy? Think of these things with thanksgiving. You know what other two things cannot be held in the mind at the same time? Gratitude and hopelessness. Studies show that gratitude actually alters the brain.

If your conflict is with another, do they have all of the facts? How were they feeling just before the conflict arose? People often react situationally. Their reaction may not be about you at all. Not everything is personal, though we often take things personally. Just like people say not to take your work home, but you think about work at home and worry about personal affairs at work (the Spillover-Crossover Model), people have more things on their minds than the actual things they are doing. Ask them what they need. Sometimes that simple question can help tremendously! Now, how can you two formulate a plan to resolve the issue?

Physical

This is your opportunity to love on yourself from the outside. Touch, in all of its forms, can do wonders for your skin and self esteem. Research has shown that non sexual touching releases oxytocin, dopamine and serotonin. If you get a massage or even rub on yourself during a bath, you are giving your skin the attention it deserves. Revel in the feel of yourself and find ways to make your skin even more appealing to you. Drinking water, moisturizing, body scrubs, and applying SPF is a great way to take care of your outer layer. Foot rubs, mani or pedicures where they massage those parts, or full body massages are all fantastic ways of honoring your body.

We know that exercise and diet are important, and yes, you should absolutely find ways of moving daily; but sometimes, we just want a cupcake. Go eat that cupcake! Savor it. Roll it around in your mouth and let your tastebuds sing. You deserve that pleasure. Then go love on yourself in another way.

Non-sexual touching, like holding hands, pats on the back, rubbing tension out of shoulders, etc, are excellent ways to connect with others. When having a baby, you are advised that babies need skin on skin contact. So do all ages. Studies have shown that when you don't get enough physical touch, you can become stressed, anxious, or depressed. As a response to stress, your body makes a hormone called cortisol. This can cause your heart rate, blood pressure, muscle tension, and breathing rate to go up, with bad effects for your immune and digestive systems. Romantic partners are not required for physical touch. You can give it to yourself. It can also be obtained through platonic relationships. Make it a point to touch those closest to you, with consent, of course. It will help all of you live healthier, more fulfilling lives.

Now that you understand the intimacies and how they can be applied to yourself, try to determine which is best for you. Just like everyone has a top Love Language, but others that are very close, so too, do you have preferred intimacies. What soothes you the most? Do you find yourself feeling most confident after you have read a new book, created something, spoken affirmations, run a mile? Knowing what is most impactful is important for your overall well being, as well as, your connection with others. It can be the way easiest way to bond with others and help yourself through darker periods. Try leaning into an intimacy and discovering how amazing you really are!

When you know your wants and needs, you can define the rules in your relationship. If one or both people don't know what they need, things get overlooked. And that's where resentment comes to play. Sometimes, when our relationship with ourselves is unhealthy, we project our fantasies onto others. This leads to obstacles to building intimacy, like trying to manipulate or control the people in our lives. It can also lead to having unrealistic expectations and being disappointed when they are not met. You are now too phenomenal to live in that world any longer!

You will find you have added immeasurable gratification to your life when you apply the Intimacy Superpower to yourself. You will become more powerful and focused on finding things that bring pleasure to your life. With your newfound appreciation and respect for yourself, it will become easier to say no to things that do not serve you and yes to things that used to scare you. I know you can do it!

No New Friends?

Intimacy is important because it is **the glue that helps a relationship get through difficult times.** Intimacy encourages honesty and openness and creates opportunities for you and your partner to learn from each other and grow. Your basic human desire to be understood can be fulfilled by intimacy. Although deepening intimacy is challenging and takes time, the work done will enhance the quality of your relationship and your life.

Understanding that getting intimate with someone on one level does not necessarily guarantee intimacy on any other, eliminates the weight associated with having to be everything to everyone. I used to joke that I was "building a partner" when dating. I had one that was great for intellectual pursuits, one for sports activities, one for creative endeavors, and one for bow-chicka-bow-bow. (You definitely have to say that a certain way ;-) This was in my early twenties and before the intimacies meant very much to me. I had inadvertently begun my journey towards this book.

Some people have friends for many years and others have to get a new set every few years. Keeping friendships and even more so making new friends, while in your adult years is much more difficult than it should be. Here are ways to keep your friends close, secure new ones, and have healthy relationships with your family and everyone else in your circle.

Essential ingredients for intimacy:
1. Compassion. Compassion is unconditional love and empathy. It's understanding that you and your person are two humans doing the best you can.

2. Trust. Both parties trust they can go to the other. Both trust that the other's love is unconditional.

3. Honesty. Honesty is the foundation of that deeper level of closeness. You can tell your friend/partner your deepest secrets and trust they will still love you unconditionally.

4. Communication. As you get more comfortable sharing things with your friend/partner, intimacy naturally develops.

5. Affection. You can develop that closeness from intimacy through affection. Affection can be shown in different ways, like hugs, kisses and cuddles.

6. Mutual Responsibility. Building intimacy will take work, commitment, and responsibility from both parties. There will be some days where one will need to carry more responsibility than the other. Overall, there should be a mutual commitment to getting closer.

9 *Obstacles to Building Intimacy*

Intimacy requires love, time, and care. It can be watered like a plant - but in order to grow, this plant needs to be watered by both partners.

Getting to know each other and building closeness sounds easy. But the reality is that humans, even though some believe so, are not perfect. The path to intimacy will have obstacles.

Some people have trouble building intimacy because they fear losing their sense of independence. On the other hand, some can have trouble with intimacy because they focus on fixing their partner rather than accepting them. Obstructions like these and others can show up and stand in the way of true intimacy. When you notice any of the following, try to nip them in the bud. Remembering why you love your partner will help keep you going as you overcome these barriers to building intimacy together.

Avoid or remove these obstacles:

1. Trapping yourself in routine. Your relationship might reach a point where everything becomes routine. You find yourself at the same restaurants, repeating conversations, doing the same weekend activities. Getting trapped in that routine can plateau the level of intimacy you have with your partner.

- Surprise your partner with a date in a new location.
- Choose a new hobby to pick up together.

2. Building walls. During an argument, you might have the tendency to shut down and stop communicating with your partner. If that happens, step away, take a break and return to the conversation later.

- Calmly let your partner know that you need a break from the conversation.

- Studies have shown that a 20-30 minute break can change an entire situation. Take that time.
- Revisit the conversation with your partner.

3. Fear of intimacy. A subconscious fear of intimacy can prevent you from getting closer to your partner. You might have difficulty communicating your own needs or have a tendency to sabotage the relationships you enter.

- Identify where the fear comes from. Are you scared of being hurt?
- Set boundaries to feel safe.
- Communicate your feelings.

4. Lack of time. You might find yourself prioritizing other things above your relationship. If you struggle with time, pay attention to what's been prioritized above the relationship.

- Schedule regular date nights and times to check in with your partner.

5. Dishonesty. True intimacy cannot be built if there are secrets or dishonesty in a relationship.

Dishonesty might show up from a fear of the closeness and vulnerability that comes from honesty. If this is the case for you, keep in mind that honesty will bring you closer to your partner.

- Be transparent with your feelings.
- Create a safe space for both of you to share uncomfortable truths.

6. Aggression. Aggression might indicate a lack of respect in the relationship. Being aggressive, critical, or showing contempt is a flag that should be taken seriously.

- Build a culture of appreciation. Go out of your way to let your partner know how much you appreciate them.

7. Doubtfulness or lack of trust. Couples might have a hard time trusting because of past issues or something their partner has done. It's important to address any lack of trust because intimacy is unobtainable without it.

8. Control. Sometimes we subconsciously try to control what happens in the relationship or how our partner feels. This can be an obstacle to intimacy. We have to let go of our desire to control in order to experience true intimacy.

9. Avoidance. Maybe you want to avoid a topic that needs to be addressed or avoid having a difficult conversation. Intimacy cannot flourish in this environment. Please speak.

You might notice these obstacles are very human! They will pop up and occur naturally. Do your best to be cognizant of them and remove them from your relationship. When you do this and follow the exercises in this book, you can experience the love and joy possible from true, deep intimacy.

Couple looking away from each other.
Doing the exercises in this book will help you
move beyond this situation.

A Life of Love Letters

Letters between one of America's Founding Fathers, John Adams and wife, Abigail Adams. *"And there is a tye more binding than Humanity, and stronger than Friendship … unite these, and there is a threefold chord — and by this chord I am not ashamed to say that I am bound, nor do I [believe] that you are wholly free from it."* • And nearly 20 years later, *"…should I draw you the picture of my Heart, it would be what I hope you still would Love; tho it contained nothing new; the early possession you obtained there; and the absolute power you have ever maintained over it; leaves not the smallest space unoccupied."*

From John, *"I want to hear you think, or see your Thoughts."*

The respect and adoration they shared never diminished. *"I look back to the early days of our acquaintance; and Friendship, as to the days of Love and Innocence; and with an indescribable pleasure I have seen near a score of years roll over our Heads, with an affection heightened and improved by time — nor have the dreary years of absence in the smallest degree effaced from my mind the Image of the dear untitled man to whom I gave my Heart…"* •

After 34 years of marriage, John said, *"It is fit and proper that you and I should retire together and not one before the other. I am with unabated confidence and affection yours…"* John and Abigail Adams were married for over 50 years, had six children (though only four lived to adulthood), helped found a country, were the first couple to live in the White House, and still gave us such a great love story.

The Beginning of a Great Love Story

The rush felt at the start of a relationship is exciting, invigorating. You are getting to know someone new, trying new things, perhaps discovering something about yourself. You are filled with many emotions, curiosity, hope, anxiety, excitement, insert emotion here _____. It is a situation unlike any other. This feeling, the Honeymoon Phase, is glorious! It also, unfortunately, does not last forever. Many people begin wondering, how can I continue growing closer to this person now that the rose colored excitement has begun to fade?

I bet you can guess the answer! Deepening the intimacy in your relationship is the best way to get closer to anyone, your partner, a family member, yourself. As mentioned earlier, intimacy is not about sex.

It is the closeness and connection you feel with someone else. Just like you can have sex without intimacy, you can have intimacy without sex. In a relationship, intimacy is how you cultivate your love and desire for someone. It is the glue that keeps relationships together after the initial spark fades, a closeness that builds over time. It is that safe space where you can be vulnerable, open, understood, accepted.

Maintaining and growing intimacy takes work, intention and time. The payoff? It creates opportunities for you and your partner to learn from each other and grow. Strengthening your bond to an entirely new, incomparable level. Utilizing these intimacies allows you to explore the whole of one another and fall in love with parts you may not have even known were there. Let us discuss each intimacy as it relates to a romantic/ life partner and the one crucial thing required for all of the intimacies, not to mention the ultimate success of your relationship.

What is that one thing?

There are some people who put their money in institutions because they do not trust people, while others hide it in their mattress/home safe/X marks the spot burial because they do not trust institutions. Both sets of people can be right. When you are guarding your heart, it is usually because people and/or someone involved in the institutions of marriage/family/religion have hurt you in some way. Why trust either? I am here to tell you that taking a chance on your future happiness is always worth it.

Can you keep a secret? Are you trustworthy? Before trying to build a relationship, it is something you should honestly self-assess. Emotions are serious business. Wars have been fought over them. Likewise, masterpieces have been created and people united because of them. Trust, dear friend, is a fragile thing. Are you worthy?

The foundation for a relationship's intimacy is rooted in trust. It should be forged without projections, expectations, or trying to control the other person. Trust is built by being reliable and showing up to the relationship as a teammate.

David Richo, author of How to Be An Adult in a Relationship, gives Five A's of a Loving Relationship and I will share them with you to help you on your journey of establishing trust. If you integrate them into your regular routine, you will find it much easier to build trust and enjoy your partner. We will build upon these going forward. The rewards are endless!

1. Attention. Connect and give your partner attention. To do this we must listen, but also minimize distractions.

2. Acceptance. Accept your partner as they are instead of trying to change them or judge them. Respect who they are as an individual.

3. Appreciation. Create a culture of appreciation as an alternative to aggression or resentment. Do not take your partner for granted.

4. Affection. Give your partner affection unconditionally through words and actions.

5. Allowing. Let go of any nature to control your partner. Give them space to explore their interests and friendships. Allow your partner to be free and they can show up as their best selves for you.

Here are other ways to build trust:

1. Keep agreements. Be reliable. Show your partner that they can trust your word.

2. Support your beloved. This will show your partner that they can rely on you for support.

3. Take care of yourself, but never at the expense of your partner or others. This will show your partner that you are not their responsibility but their partner.

4. Respect each other's boundaries. We have boundaries that show others how we are willing to be treated. Avoiding stepping over established lines shows both compassion and respect.

5. Listen without judgment. This will create a safe space in the relationship.

There is that phrase again, Safe Space. Let's talk about it.

Emotionally Safe Spaces

E motional intimacy is building closeness. It is connecting through actions that express vulnerability and trust. It's that safe space you create to share your deepest thoughts and feelings with each other. One does not simply will a safe space into being. It is built brick by brick through experience and intention.

How does one begin to build a safe space? At the beginning of my group sessions, I say, "This is a Judgement Free Zone and Safe Space;" but, does me saying it make it so? Not at all. The entire process of these sessions allows for the group to establish it. It is an expectation: esteemed, enforced, exemplified, and ultimately achieved.

Let us break down each requirement. When creating a safe space, we must first understand it. It does not require a secret meeting place with the words Safe Space chiseled upon the entryway, but is an expectation both parties hold for one another. It becomes an unspoken (or spoken) agreement between us, your secrets are safe, vulnerability treasured, honesty encouraged, point of view respected, and feelings valid. In addition, my responses to you will be rooted in love. These things are held in the highest regard. We vow not to throw stones for fear of cracking this fragile trust we are forging. When these traits are mirrored to one another, it is simple to shape a space conducive to fostering emotional intimacy.

What can you do to encourage emotional intimacy? The first thing that must be accepted is that this may take time, just like trust. Love is patient. Most people enjoy talking about themselves, but the vulnerable parts take a little coaxing. Eventually, they will open up to you. If you are able to display authenticity and vulnerability, they will be more apt to do so as well. Again, our responses should be rooted in love.

The best way to have in-depth conversations is active listening. If needed, refer to the Connections section for a refresher on active listening.

Emotional Intimacy is enhanced by honest conversations. It is oftentimes scary to be vulnerable to others. But when you are open to sharing your truth, others will likely follow suit.

Here are a few exercises you can do to encourage growth in the area of Emotional Intimacy.

1. When having in-depth conversations, practice non-judgmental listening. Breathe before responding. Some things do not require a response at all.
2. Ask one another questions about childhood, particularly the stories you do not normally share.

3. Share an exhausting work situation and each allow the other to fully express themselves.
4. Discuss your hopes, fears, and/or goals.
5. Discuss fetishes or secret desires in an open, non-judgmental way.
6. Talk about something that deeply hurt or scarred you.

Cute, smart, rich -
But are you available?
I mean emotionally.

Intellectual Connection

There's nothing quite like connecting with someone on a deep, intellectual level. It's like a beautiful dance between minds, a tango of thoughts and ideas. First things first, let's define what intellectual intimacy with another actually means. It's essentially when you share a deep, meaningful connection with someone based on your intellectual compatibility. You don't have to agree on everything, but you do have to be able to challenge and inspire each other in a way that stimulates your brains. Intellectual intimacy is getting to know how your partner's mind works. Ideas, thoughts, and opinions … and accepting differences of opinions.

Some people might think that intellectual intimacy requires being serious and scholarly at all times. But that couldn't be further from the truth! In fact, it can be incredibly fun and flirty. When you're engaged in a stimulating conversation with someone, there's a natural energy that arises, a spark that can ignite all kinds of playful banter and witty repartee. Think about it - have you ever had a conversation with someone where you just clicked, where the words flowed effortlessly and you found yourself laughing and smiling the whole time? That's intellectual intimacy, my friend. It's like having a mental playdate with someone who just gets you.

And let's be real - there are few things sexier than being with someone who challenges you intellectually. When you're able to have deep, meaningful conversations with another, it creates a bond that's unlike anything else. It opens an entirely new side of them, one that's vulnerable, authentic and real.

So, how do you cultivate intellectual intimacy with someone? Well, it all starts with being open and curious. You have to be willing to explore new ideas and perspectives, and a desire to listen to what the other person has to say. That means being present in the moment, not just waiting for your turn to speak.

It is also important to be vulnerable. Share your thoughts and opinions openly, even if they're unpopular or controversial. That's what creates a space for real connection - when you're willing to be honest and authentic with someone, it opens the door to a deeper level of understanding.

And don't be afraid to play! Intellectual intimacy doesn't have to be serious all the time. In fact, some of the best conversations come from a place of playfulness and humor. So don't be afraid to crack a joke or tease each other a bit. It's all part of the fun.

Of course, not everyone is going to be a perfect match for you when it comes to intellectual intimacy. And that's okay! It's important to find someone who complements you intellectually, not necessarily someone who agrees with everything you say. So don't be afraid to keep searching until you find that special someone who lights up your brain in all the right ways.

Many people have said that I make them feel more intelligent. This is because of a few reasons: 1. I meet them where they are. Whatever their personal beliefs or knowledge of a situation, I begin there. Since people usually approach me for my expertise, education, and experience, they are in learning mode. I am there to stimulate them intellectually. 2. I ask questions and help them figure out solutions to their problems. While I do give information, I mostly help them help themselves. There is a special bond that is created when you are involved in a "lightbulb moment." When dealing with Intellectual Intimacy, it is important to share knowledge, wisdom, ideas, etc, but it more important to help someone else gain something and feel seen. Try it! You are an expert in something, I promise!

When you are free to share personal philosophies and give opinions, especially if they differ, and are still met with love, you have Intellectual Intimacy. This is the feeling of "they get me!" and is truly wondrous. This intimacy is enhanced by sharing diverging thoughts, innermost secrets and new ideas. Who knows - you might just find your mental soulmate.

Here are a few exercises you can do to develop Intellectual Intimacy with another.

1. Try one another's hobbies
2. Create a list of interesting topics and randomly bring up one for engaging conversations.
3. Discuss movies after watching them.
4. Talk about core values.
5. Ask their opinion about various issues, both trivial and deep. (Safe space)

**Ideas converge,
dance minds intertwined, find rhythm
cerebral bonding**

Some specific questions you can use to encourage Emotional and Intellectual Intimacy

- How do you think you have grown in the past five years?
- How do you want to grow in the next five years?
- What are three qualities you admire about yourself?
- What is something you've always wanted to do, but haven't done yet? Why not?
- Tell me about one of the happiest days of your life.
- What is one of the most embarrassing moments of your life?
- What's your fondest childhood memory?
- Which small romantic gestures would you like more of?
- Tell me about what the perfect career looks like to you.
- What traits do you value in a friend?
- What do you need to feel happy and fulfilled?
- How are you doing, really?
- What is missing from the relationship?
- How can I support your growth?

Experience Life Together

Think of every action movie/love story you've ever seen. The action hero and person being saved go through several car chases, a few fight scenes, maybe a shootout or two and fall in love in the course of a few days. For some, this is Hollywood fiction at its finest; but, what if I told you that it has some scientific support? People bond through shared experiences. If those experiences are harrowing, it is exponential.

Basic training, war, rushing a fraternity or sorority, football or any other team sport, and trauma are all examples of experiences that bond persons to one another. If you do not have these options, no worries. We will discuss ways to implement experiential intimacy into your relationships.

There have been numerous experiments between strangers that gauge attraction. In each study, potential couples are put into date simulations, one being dinner, another a more active outing, such as walks on the beach, and the final being something more dangerous or stressful like walking a tightrope bridge or couple's skydiving. In EVERY experiment, the attraction to the potential mate was found in the most stressful situation, if handled properly. For you, this means choosing dates that make you sweat in some way, even if it is emotionally or intellectually. You learn a lot about a person in these cases. You also find yourself relying on one another, which builds immediate trust. What is the most important thing in these intimacies? You can accelerate the time it normally takes to achieve it. You just became a Speedster!

To build Experiential Intimacy into your relationships, find something you both enjoy. It could be anything. Oftentimes, the funniest stories happen during normal outings when something out of the ordinary happens. There are not ways to get those if you do not make time to connect with your people in real life. You can try tabletop games, either cooperative or competitive. Tip: Cooperative is MUCH safer! You should also try something outside of the norm. There is nothing like something that stretches the imagination or activates the nerves to make a great story. And in the end, those are the memories that are told over laughter, good meals, and reunions. You influenced that. You are indeed powerful.

Laughter and tears
Adventures shared in tandem
Memories forever

Creative Pursuits

While it is easy to wish for superhuman strength or flight ability, one can see how important creativity can be if we look at Batman or Iron Man. Both are human, but use their creative minds to stand shoulder to shoulder with aliens and gods. While you may not need shark repellant or a Hulk Smashing suit, your creativity can indeed change lives.

Creative Intimacy has the power to outlive the creators. Immortality! Since I am sure you already explored your personal creative powers in previous chapters, let's try to share it.

I have always been an introvert. My passions are traditionally individual pursuits, reading, writing, daydreaming of ways to save the world. That being the case, when I decided to share my writing, poetry especially, I found that others were moved by it. I have heard "I don't feel so alone" quite often. How can I stop sharing when it expands someone else's life? What if I allowed fear to keep me from my destiny? Performing on stages all over the world would have never materialized. I could not have reached so many people with my art. Also, I never would have met the people who have become so important to my creative life!

Sharing your creative works can be scary. As Erykah Badu said, "I am an artist and I'm sensitive about my sh!t!" As we have discussed, these intimacies require vulnerability. There is strength in that! Are you a painter, sculptor, writer, comedian, dancer, rock climber, mime? Have you ever tried combining your passion with another's? You do not have to have the same talent. Build something new and magical! Sharing something this close to both of your hearts creates a special type of bond. I believe in your power!

Here are a few exercises you can do to develop Creative Intimacy with another.

1. Create a couple's vision board
2. Create a joint comic strip. You can create characters modeled after the two of you and others you know. This can also help in difficult situations because the characters can speak for you when you are not quite sure how to approach your partner.
3. A couple's journal! You can leave a book in a specific spot and write notes to each other or choose different days of the week to add your own entries. This can also be used to create entries together to a prompt. You can also use a digital version.

Spiritual Intimacy

Spiritual Intimacy was one of the most difficult for me, or should I say, most difficult to find. I grew up in a Christian church, spend many evenings in Bible Study or choir rehearsal, Sundays in Sunday school and church, and weekends at youth retreats. Most of my friends were made in church, and I seriously considered going into the seminary. Even though I dated partners found in church, I did not feel an intimate spiritual connection with them. As I got older and found myself more spiritual and less religious, I dated a variety of people from various backgrounds, Seventh Day Adventist, Baptist, Muslim, Catholic, Atheist, Agnostic, Buddhist, Yoruba, nondenominational. I have prayed for partners, prayed with partners, attended religious services together and still not felt what I considered a spiritual intimacy with them.

Though I have studied intimacy for many years, this particular one eluded me. The very definition given by historians and leading researchers in the field would say that my actions constituted sharing a spiritual intimacy. They would tell me that my partners derived satisfaction from the moments we shared and memories we created. We built a closeness through prayer and attendance that cannot be denied. It is interesting that I wanted more. I was not sure what "more" looked like, but that did not stop me from wanting it!

When I was young, I felt God within me. I was absolutely confident in this fact. I felt a love and peace that could not be explained. There were various experiences that happened over the course of my life that lead me to believe in the blessings of the Universe. Those experiences could probably fill another book. Though not religious, I tell you all of this to convey that I am connected with my soul, spirit, the little voice in my head that whispers, whatever you may call it. When it speaks, I listen.

One day, I met a person. When I got close to them, I felt my spirit reach out for them. I had never had that happen before. It was a strange, but not unappealing, sensation. Though I was unsure as to the why, I listened. This person literally changed my life. The experiences we have shared defy explanation and are the very "more" I did not know I was still looking for. A Spiritual Intimacy hits differently than the others. In fact, each intimacy causes different parts of you to react, making the connection deeper in a multitude of ways.

To obtain Spiritual Intimacy with another, psychic powers are unnecessary and it has nothing to do with religion. This is why couples of differing religions can have deeply rewarding and successful relationships. To begin building this intimacy, let us start with the basics.

The questions you must ask yourself before embarking on this journey are: What are your beliefs about the world, the spiritual realm, your relation to it? What does spirituality mean to you? It can be attendance at a temple, mosque, church, etc, or it can be that you do not believe in a God at all. As you see, there are no right and wrong answers as it pertains to your truth. But you must stand in it, whatever that may be.

Once you know yourself, you can expand to others. Is praying daily with your partner important to you? Is being outdoors during the solstice and performing rituals during this key time part of your belief? Perhaps it is meditating, or doing positive affirmations in the mornings or maybe it is them seeing the god in you. A spiritual connection feels comfortable and familiar, even if you just met. They have the ability to calm you , even in thought. If you have achieved this independently by learning to control your inner self, be careful! You can give off Soulmate Energy vibes to innocent bystanders!

Here are some exercises to grow your Spiritual Intimacy with another:

1. Meditate together. It is fine if your mind wanders, just acknowledge the thought without judgement and move on. Be present in your body and mind. Discuss how you feel afterwards.

2. Discuss your views on spirituality. Be open and honest. Remember that you have created a Safe Space.

3. Soul Gazing: Sit down facing your partner, as close as you can comfortably. (If you can touch foreheads and breathe together, even better) Look into each other's eyes for five minutes. Yes, you can blink. This is not a staring contest. Warning, this will be uncomfortable. Do not look away! You will see the depths of yourself as well as your partner. Process what you saw and felt. Then feel free to discuss when you are ready. It need not be the same day.

Sacred energy
Heart and spirit intertwined
Two souls connected

Conflict is Good?

Ah, the most difficult, but rewarding of all of the intimacies. Sometimes it would be great to have Professor X, Poison Ivy, or Killgrave (Purple Man) powers and just get people to do what we want. Sigh. Since we will inevitably run into conflict with another human, it is best to be prepared.

Building intimacy and falling in love feels easy. Knowing how to keep the love alive does not feel as natural. It is easy to either give up on the relationship when things get hard or settle because you love your partner.

Remember that disagreements are unavoidable. What you can control is the way you respond to conflict. Instead of settling when things get hard, the disagreements you have can become a way for you to understand each other better, learn, and grow.

When you learn how to build intimacy beyond conflict, you'll see that the content of the disagreements isn't what's most important. You will discover the most critical things are the following:

- The way you respond
- What your triggers/patterns are
- How you resolve the conflict
- Listening can be a demonstration of love

As mentioned in the self empowerment Conflict section, here are five suggestions that will work **during the moment** conflict arises.

1. Be silent if you cannot say it without screaming.
2. Be silent when you are feeling critical.
3. Be silent in the heat of anger.
4. Be silent when you do not have all of the facts.
5. Breathe. Breathe. Breathe. Then speak

I know these are the exact opposite of what you would like to do when angry, but saying something destructive is much, much worse! Let us learn to use this time to decide what is important to us. With each breath, remember why you love your partner(s). Also remember that you are stronger than this moment.

Studies have shown that the couples that last longest are not the ones that do not fight. They are the ones who understand that they will weather this storm. They have learned how to fight fair and accept the lessons. Once you understand that no one individually "wins" in a couple argument, life becomes much easier. You are a team and will do what is best for the team. We saw how difficult it was for the Avengers to work together as a team, but we all know that "Earth's Mightiest Heroes" were stronger together, just like you and your partner(s).

Let us discuss fighting fair. When angry it is easy to lash out. Depending on your past experiences, conflict can cause a multitude of emotions. Use the Emotion Wheel when conflict arises to determine exactly how you are feeling and the corresponding actions that often accompany it. That will help you understand why you (or your partner) are reacting a certain way. Once you understand something, you can work to combat the negative aspects.

When discussing something you and you partner disagree on, try to stick to the actual topic. When cornered or if you feel like you are "losing," it is easy to lapse into Four Horseman (chapter 4) behavior that does not improve the situation.

As a refresher, the Four Horseman of Conflict are Criticism, Contempt, Defensiveness and Stonewalling. Let us now discuss the antidotes. Criticism: The antidote is Gentle Start Up. It uses feelings , "I" statements, and a positive need. For example: Criticism - "You always do _____. You're so selfish!"

Gentle Start Up - "I feel hurt/scared/unseen/ unimportant/etc when you do _____. I would love it if we could do _____ instead." Using the second example, an action can be taken to alleviate the issue without resorting to attacking the person's character.

Contempt: Besides being the single greatest indicator of divorce, couples who engage in contemptuous behavior have been found to suffer from illnesses (colds, flu, etc.) more often. The antidote is in-depth expressions of desires and appreciation. Since contempt is used to make another feel demoralized and worthless, the only way to combat that is to show your appreciation and fondness for your partner. Acknowledge their strengths and give compliments. If there is a specific issue, it needs to be discussed in great detail. Instead of eye rolling, dismissive attitudes and severe name calling, try searching for ways to brainstorm solutions. Also, make time to analyze your behavior to see why you are acting this way.

Defensiveness: The antidote is Taking Responsibility. It requires one to own up to their behaviors, avoid taking feedback personally and show remorse and apologize. For example: Defensiveness - "It isn't my fault I yelled. You were late, not me!"

Responsibility - "I shouldn't have raised my voice at you. I'm sorry." The second example shows your partner you acknowledge their feelings and do not want to hurt them. You can discuss the lateness afterwards with a Gentle Start Up.

Stonewalling: The antidote is Self-Soothing. Use relaxation techniques to calm down and stay present with your partner. If your natural reaction is to go silent or withdraw, you must find ways to gather yourself. Often this is a result of past trauma, either prior to the relationship or the result of the first Three Horseman used frequently. It can be difficult to have a rational discussion at this point. Ask to take a break, confirming it is simply a pause. Then spend 20 minutes doing something to self-sooth, taking a walk, breathing deeply, reading a book, taking a shower, positive affirmations, whatever works for you. Finally, return with a desire to discuss, listen and discover solutions. Remember to breathe during the discussion.

Each of these activities have one thing in common. They are geared towards making a positive step after the discussion. If you are both actively listening and being authentic, you can emerge even stronger than you were before the disagreement. This is the beauty of Conflict Intimacy. You are forging an unbreakable bond because you both know that whatever the circumstance, you two can emerge victorious over the problem. That is true power!

Passionate clashes
Intimate insights revealed
Conflict as bonding

Bow Chicka Bow Bow

You definitely have to say that a certain way!

I know I have said that intimacy does not mean sex, but sometimes it does! Though there are so many ways to grow physical intimacy without sex, you are probably not here for the hand holding, hugging, and pats on the back. Those things are important. You should definitely take time to intentionally hug your partner for several seconds. It inspires connection. You should also rub their booty occasionally.

There are many ways to build physical intimacy that leads to better sex, like kissing, cuddling, and massages. These things should be done whether or not sex is an option at the moment. If not, it leads to resentment and that is a sure fire way NOT to have sex!

Now, onto the sex! Well, not so fast. Physical intimacy is best achieved after conversations. Just like every other intimacy involves authenticity and vulnerability, this one is no different. Given that there is an orgasm gap* and I have crowned myself its greatest nemesis, we must talk! What does it for you, sexually? Have you explored your body over the years? Or allowed someone else to do it? Even if you have, you change regularly. What worked with someone else may not work with your new partner. And I am not just talking about them! You will respond differently to this new person. And by new, I mean every person is a completely new shell every seven years.

Over the years in my coaching business, I have met people who have never had sex, only been with one partner and who are very free spirits. From those who only like to masturbate to those with multiple partners, we all enjoy the feeling of freedom. That is what sex is, at its core. You are free to explore your deepest desires and see them manifested with pleasure (and a pain mixture, if that is your thing!) in real time. The French term, La petite mort, the little death, refers to orgasm. Philosophers have suggested that term is most accurate because orgasm causes not only a physical liberation, but a spiritual one as well. If nothing else, it is a wonderful reminder that we are indeed, still alive! Though the best physical and sexual intimacies do not solely focus on the destination, it is a great thing when you arrive!

Let us discuss the journey. For the best growth of physical intimacy, one should have a never ending curiosity and desire. A curiosity about both you and your partner's bodies and a desire to bring them increased pleasure daily. This does not have to mean sex daily, but a giving of pleasure. It could be something as simple as deep, sensual kisses that take your breath away to long sexual sessions that leave you dehydrated and ready for the best sleep of your life. Either way, you are giving gratification to your partner and self. This is an intimacy that cannot be grown by focusing on self. One must be truly committed to the celebration and satisfaction of their partner.

You two have shared hopes, dreams, traumas, experiences, issues, everything; but, for many, discussing sexual interests and desires, proclivities and private moments, are nearly impossible. It is the last taboo of American society, along with many other cultures. I am here to give you permission to embark on that mission. Ask one another about sensitive places, deep desires and bucket lists. Ask if there is something they have done, heard about, saw in a movie that they would like to try. And DO NOT JUDGE! This requires a safe space too!

When you have heard what your partner desires, you should ... wait for it... wait for it... Try it! I know, I know. It is a novel idea, but hear me out. Many couples I have coached do not try it. They judge it. One party says absolutely not to the other's wants.

Now, perhaps because I am an open minded, curious, free spirited type of person, "absolutely not" is not typically a part of my sexual vocabulary. That being said, I can understand it. If it is something you have been taught is dirty, beneath you, sinful, etc., I get it. I am here to tell you that most of what you have been taught regarding sexual interaction is rooted in fear, patriarchy and ignorance. I may go into a very detailed descriptions on why this is the case in another book, but, it is nevertheless, true. Why base your pleasure, or lack thereof, on someone else's ideas of right and wrong? Just like cocaine was fine in Coca Cola and lead was used in paint, right and wrong change.

Opening yourself sexually can be scary. Just like the other intimacies, it takes an extreme amount of trust to not just share your ideas and private thoughts, but body as well. It is a sharing of energy unlike the others. And cultivating an intimacy unlike any you have had before will require you to do things you have not attempted previously. (I am sure you just thought of something that I would love to discuss with you in a session!) By something new, I mean being more open. Your heart, mind, spirit and body should be included. Everything that you have worked on in this book will come into play for you to experience the most mind blowing sexual adventure of your life. And if you have mastered the steps in the self intimacy section, you will be snatching souls in no time!

Here are some exercises to enhance your physical and sexual intimacy. In each exercise we are looking for a few things that enhance a healthy sexual experience...

- Attunement: to your and your partner's body
- Creativity: A key to fantastic sex is creating space for creativity.
- Presence: the practice of being present and making room for the various emotions and spontaneous desires.
- Self Advocacy: sharing what you like, did not enjoy, and what you want more of.

- Intimacy, of course!

1. Body mapping: This requires you to cover every inch of your partner. You will be taking notes on their reaction to your touch, changes in pressure and whether they respond best to fingers, tongue, or some other extremity or accessory. Use steps from the next exercise.

2. Sensory Play: This can be used with Body Mapping, if so desired. Sensory Play requires props, so you must prepare. You will need items of varying hard and softness, as well as things of varying temperatures. A blindfold and earplugs are wonderful additions. For example: feather, silk or satin items, something stainless steel to go in the freezer, a candle, hot wax, massage oil, a vibrator. (You can also add more BDSM friendly items like floggers, Wartenburg wheels, crops, nipple clamps, paddles, violet wands.)
   - Find a comfortable space and decide who is going to be the giver and the receiver.

Blindfold the receiver. The giver then chooses an item. Think of the receiver's body in sections, upper arm, lower arm, upper thigh, lower leg, chest, midsection, etc.

- Beginning with the chosen section and item, use it with varying degrees of pressure and movement. For example, the feather with light pressure in circles or more pressure with long strokes. See how each feels on each part of the body. Check in with the receiver with every change, be it pressure, movement , body section or item. Take notes! Remember, this is not about orgasm, but learning the other's body. One generally avoids the most intimate areas during Sensory Play and Body Mapping, but it is your party. Do what you want!

- Those familiar with BDSM will understand what happens next. The giver then gives the receiver "aftercare." In lifestyle scenes this is many people's favorite part! It means to check in with your partner post-play. It can be rubbing on the receiver, say petting them or massaging their scalp, reassuring them in some way, but ALWAYS talking about the session. Your aftercare can be anything that makes you happy. After this step, you two can switch and the giver becomes the receiver.

3. 20 Minute Sensual Meeting: This is when sex would be inappropriate or you are not comfortable with the more detailed exercises. Take 5 minutes to gaze into each other's eyes and breathe deeply together. The next 5 minutes are spent caressing your partner's limbs, face, neck, torso. The next 5 minutes you allow them to do the same to you. The last 5 minutes are spent kissing. You can, of course, use this as a precursor to an intimate evening or when trying to rekindle the passion after some quiet weeks or months. If you are looking to rekindle your romance immediately, do

the exercises in the Spiritual Intimacy section as well.

Skin on skin, we breathe
Connect, touch, ignite the soul
Electricity

Too Much?

Intimacy is an essential part of human relationships. However, as with anything in life, there can be too much of a good thing. While intimacy is generally seen as a positive aspect of relationships, there is a point where it can become too much. Let us explore whether there is such a thing as too much intimacy in relationships.

Since intimacy is not just about physical closeness, but also emotional closeness, which includes trust, vulnerability, and communication; it has the potential to become a villain. While it helps you feel loved, secure, and emotionally fulfilled, there is a point where too much intimacy can become suffocating and even damaging to the relationship.

One of the downsides of too much intimacy is a loss of personal space. When partners spend too much time together and share every aspect of their lives, it can become challenging to maintain a sense of independence. This can be particularly problematic if one partner is more dependent on the other for emotional support or has a more dominant personality. The other partner may feel stifled or unable to assert themselves, leading to a breakdown in the relationship.

Another issue with too much intimacy is that it can lead to a lack of mystery or excitement in the relationship. When partners know everything about each other, there may be fewer surprises or opportunities for growth. It can be challenging to maintain the passion and excitement that comes with the early stages of a relationship when partners are constantly in each other's company and know everything about one another. This can lead to boredom, frustration, and even resentment.

Furthermore, too much intimacy can lead to a lack of privacy. When partners share everything with each other, including their deepest fears and insecurities, it can be challenging to maintain boundaries. This can lead to a loss of individuality and a feeling of being constantly exposed. It can also lead to a sense of mistrust if one partner feels that the other is not respecting their boundaries or keeping their secrets.

However, it is essential to note that intimacy levels differ from person to person. Some people thrive on constant emotional and physical closeness, while others need more space and independence. Therefore, what constitutes too much intimacy varies from relationship to relationship. What might be too much for one person might be just the right amount for another.

Here are some signs that too much intimacy is becoming a problem in a relationship. One of the most significant indicators is a loss of individuality. If partners are spending all their time together, it can be challenging to maintain separate interests, hobbies, and friendships. This can lead to a sense of co-dependency and a loss of personal identity. If partners find that they no longer have any individual interests or hobbies, it may be a sign that they are spending too much time together.

Another sign that intimacy levels are becoming problematic is a loss of communication. When partners are too close, it can be challenging to speak openly and honestly with each other. This can lead to a lack of trust and a breakdown in the relationship. If partners find that they are no longer communicating effectively, it may be a sign that they need to take a step back and reevaluate their level of intimacy.

Finally, another indication that intimacy levels are becoming an issue is a lack of physical intimacy. While too much physical intimacy can sometimes be suffocating, a lack of physical intimacy can be equally damaging. If partners find that they are no longer physically attracted to each other or have lost interest in sex, it may be a sign that their intimacy levels have become too low.

The remedy? Honest communication. Let your partner know how you feel. You may need to find a new hobby or interest group. This is not because of a deficiency in your partner (please let them know this!), but a need for your personal development. Your growth can encourage them to explore other avenues as well. This will give you a few things: new topics to discuss, time away to miss one another, new ideas for your future together. Since you understand the intimacies, especially conflict, this is simply another way to grow together.

The Power of Practice

The Conclusion?

Building intimacy with your partner can be the way to rekindle the fire you felt at the beginning of the relationship. The happiest couples are those who have intentionally built on all seven levels of intimacy. Here are a few more suggestions for ways to incorporate intimacy building into your daily life. It doesn't have to be big or time consuming. Consistent practice of your newfound superpowers will pay big dividends on your happiness.

1. **Respond to your partner's signals.** Notice when your partner reaches out to you. This might show up in simple ways, like a smile or suggestion. Turn towards your partner for connection.

2. **Show and tell your partner you appreciate them.** To foster a culture of appreciation, tell your partner you appreciate them!

   - "Thank you for helping with the dishes."
   - "It means a lot to me that you listen."
   - "I appreciate how supportive you are."

3. **Be affectionate to your partner based on their love language.** Do you know your partner's Love Language yet? If not, take the Quiz by Dr. Gary Chapman. Though people normally need all of them plus more, this is a simple way to tell your partner what you desire in the moment. **ALSO,** learn your "Intimacy Language" found in the quiz in this book. www.5lovelanguages.com

4. **Remember the small things.** (These things absolutely contribute to bringing you closer with your partner.)

   - Ask your partner how their day was.
   - Be playful.

- Do one act of kindness for your partner each day.

5. **Check-in weekly.** Schedule a time to check-in with your partner. Be prepared to be open and honest! This means telling your partner how feedback makes you feel (for example, maybe you feel embarrassed when they share what's missing from the relationship) instead of being defensive.

Intimacy is the most important way to nurture your relationship. At the end of the day, a happy, healthy relationship doesn't come without work. Set aside time to talk with your partner about the different levels of intimacy and what they mean to you. Discover which are most meaningful to your partner and put extra effort into their favorite. When you build a truly intimate relationship, you will grow and thrive together. You can improve the state of your relationship with a decision to commit to growing your intimacy and seeing just how powerful they can be!

Intimacy Goes To Work.

To whom it may concern…

I hope this chapter finds you well. These days, you are entering perilous waters if you bring up the word "intimacy" in the workplace. But it does not have to be that way! The stigma associated with our new favorite word is tragic! As previously discussed, we do not have to be talking about sex when using the word intimate. But that is us, dear refined reader. What about those people at your job who have not been initiated yet?

How can we bridge this gap? Well, you can always have HR give away copies of The Intimacy Superpower at the company Holiday Party or suggest I facilitate your next corporate workshop. Barring that, let us discuss why intimacy in the workplace is not just a great, but a necessary thing!

We spend one third of our life at work. When you factor in that we spend one third of it sleeping, that means that HALF, possibly more, of your waking life is spent working! Wouldn't you prefer to spend that time with people you feel connected to or at least make the environment the best it can be? Every other chapter of this book is dedicated to the rest of your life, but we want to improve all of your relationships!

Unlocking the power of intimacy in a corporate setting is like infusing a breath of fresh air into the traditional office atmosphere. Imagine a workplace where emotional connections are as valued as quarterly reports, where intellectual exchanges become the heartbeat of innovation, and shared experiences serve as the glue binding teams together. By nurturing emotional intimacy, employees forge deeper connections, fostering an environment where empathy and understanding are not just encouraged but celebrated. Intellectual intimacy, on the other hand, transforms boardrooms into vibrant think tanks, where diverse perspectives converge, and brilliant ideas emerge. This collaborative exchange of thoughts not only sparks innovation but also establishes a sense of shared purpose, aligning individual aspirations with collective goals. Adding the magic of experiential intimacy completes the trifecta, creating opportunities for team members to bond beyond the confines of daily tasks. From team-building adventures to shared successes, these experiences weave a tapestry of shared memories that elevate team morale and cohesiveness.

The impact of leveraging emotional, intellectual, and experiential intimacy in the corporate world extends far beyond mere camaraderie. A workplace imbued with these intimate elements witnesses a surge in productivity as teams find inspiration in their connections. The reduction in sick days is not just a coincidence but a testament to the strengthened immune system of a workplace where positive, intimate relationships flourish. When colleagues become more than cubicle neighbors, when they understand each other's motivations, share ideas freely, and embark on collective experiences, the result is a workplace that thrives on synergy, resilience, and a shared commitment to success. In the dance of emotions, intellect, and shared experiences, productivity becomes not just a goal but a natural outcome of a workplace culture that values the intimacy of human connections.

How do we get there?

Embedding emotional, experiential, and intellectual intimacy into a company's culture can foster a workplace environment that is not only productive but also deeply fulfilling for employees. Firstly, encouraging emotional intimacy involves creating spaces where open communication is welcomed, acknowledging and validating the emotions of team members, and fostering a culture of empathy. This can be achieved through team-building activities, regular check-ins, and leadership practices that prioritize the well-being and emotional connection of employees. Moreover, implementing experiential intimacy involves providing opportunities for shared experiences that go beyond the confines of daily tasks. Whether through team outings, collaborative projects, or skill-building workshops, these shared moments create a sense of camaraderie and shared purpose among colleagues. Lastly, nurturing intellectual intimacy calls for promoting a culture of continuous learning, collaboration, and knowledge-sharing. Encouraging brainstorming sessions, cross-functional collaborations, and investing in professional development opportunities can stimulate intellectual growth, creating a workplace where diverse ideas and perspectives are valued.

Incorporating these forms of intimacy into a company's culture not only enhances employee satisfaction but also contributes to increased innovation, improved collaboration, and a heightened sense of belonging. By prioritizing emotional, experiential, and intellectual connections, companies can build a resilient and thriving workplace culture that supports the holistic development and well-being of their teams.

Co-worker conflict?

Now, let's talk about conflict intimacy—not the kind that sparks discord but the one that fuels growth. Disagreements are inevitable, but the art lies in navigating them constructively. It's about fostering an environment where conflicting viewpoints are welcomed, respected, and channeled towards innovative solutions. This breed of intimacy not only resolves disputes but also strengthens relationships and nurtures trust within the team. Review the Conflict is Good? chapter to assist with ways to combat this pervasive issue.

Taking Work Home?

In the galactic battle between work and personal life, emotions, experiences, and stresses from one domain do not stay contained within office or home walls. Circling back to a previous chapter, let us discuss The Workplace Spillover-Crossover Theory. This model, often utilized in psychological research, paints a vivid portrait of the interconnectedness between our professional and personal realms, acknowledging that the boundaries separating these spheres are porous. For instance, the enthusiasm generated during a successful project at work might seamlessly blend into a celebratory evening with friends and/or partner(s), fueling a positive atmosphere that transcends professional boundaries. Conversely, the tranquility of a serene weekend getaway may infuse a sense of calm and focus into Monday's team meeting. This theory invites us to view the cross-pollination of experiences as a source of enrichment, where the vibrancy of one sphere enhances the other. Understanding this spillover effect becomes crucial in fostering healthy relationships, both at home and in the workplace. individual's experiences at work create waves that touch the lives of those around them.

Understanding and embracing the Workplace Spillover-Crossover Theory can lead to a more holistic approach to work and life integration. Recognizing how work experiences impact personal life allows individuals and organizations to implement strategies that mitigate negative spillover and enhance positive ones. For instance, promoting a supportive work environment, offering stress management programs, and encouraging work-life balance initiatives can significantly reduce the detrimental effects of work-related stress on personal relationships. Moreover, improving communication and empathy within relationships can help partners support each other through challenging work situations. By fostering an environment that appreciates this dynamic interplay, workplaces can become spaces where creativity, innovation, and well-being flourish.

We Don't Talk About Intimacy. No. No. No?

Corporate literature generally shies away from discussing anything intimate, however, Napoleon Hill details the exact opposite in the ever popular book, Think and Grow Rich. This classic corporate must-read, dedicates an entire chapter to sexual transmutation. Once you have connected with the intimacies for yourself, you should be ready to tackle this to become unstoppable in business.

Here are three points broken into bite sized pieces.

1. **Energy Transformation:**

   - Sexual transmutation, as outlined in Chapter 11, involves the redirection of sexual energy into more productive and creative pursuits. Instead of dissipating this potent force, individuals learn to channel it toward achieving personal and professional goals.

2. **Creative Alchemy:**

   - Napoleon Hill's concept of sexual transmutation emphasizes the alchemical process of transforming desire into creative energy. By harnessing the power of intense emotions, individuals can fuel their endeavors with heightened focus, passion, and innovation. In addition, this magnetic energy attracts opportunities, positive circumstances, and the cooperation of others.

3. **Path to Success:**

- Hill emphasizes the importance of self-discipline in mastering sexual transmutation. The ability to control and redirect one's desires requires a disciplined mind. Those who can effectively practice self-discipline in this regard are believed to unlock a powerful source of personal and professional growth.

Chapter 11 is often controversial, but the concepts have been written about and practiced for thousands of years. Learn how to do it and decide for yourself.

The Benefits of Incorporating Intimacy into Corporate Culture

- Increased productivity
- Decreased Sick Days
- Innovative ideas
- Cohesion
- Reduced HR visits
- Employee retention
- Employee satisfaction
- Elevated collaboration
- Faster implementation of new policies

Circling back, I would like to take point on your next employee bonding / corporate training / talent retention workshop. In the dynamic world of work, the connection between team members can make or break success. It's not just about synergy; it's about intimacy—the different shades of closeness that fuel collaboration and drive productivity. We're delving into a territory where emotional intelligence meets intellectual prowess, and where creative sparks ignite ingenious solutions. This can be adapted for any office environment.

Out of Office Team Building Ideas

Escape Room

Outdoor Adventure Quest

Team Cooking Class

VR Excursion

In Office Team Building Ideas

Board Game Tournament

Custom Trivia Game

Speaker Led Innovation Workshop

Team Building Through Art

For more information about The Corporate Intimacy Superpower Workshop specifically tailored to your company, visit catalystlifeglobal.com.

What is your Sexual Intimacy Language?

The following quiz was developed for my clients to discover ways to become more compatible in the bedroom. It is meant to be taken individually, then shared.

On the following pages you will find 30 sets of questions. There are two choices in each set. These exist in a vacuum, meaning that the previous and following questions do not matter. Pretend these two are the only questions being asked. Read both and choose the one that brings you the most pleasure. Think about it as if you only had those two choices. **Not the one you do most often in your current relationship or the one you know your partner enjoys; NO circle the one that most appeals to YOU**. It may be that both (or neither) apply, but please choose the one that is most meaningful or arousing to you. Sit back, relax, take your time and feel each statement. You can write down the winning letter for each set on another piece of paper if you prefer.

It is more pleasurable, satisfying, meaningful and/or arousing when ...

A I hear my partner moan during our sessions

D my partner and I switch control during the session

C my partner surprises me with an outfit for a role play session

E my partner and I touch a lot during the course of the day

B my partner takes their time kissing and caressing me

D my partner blindfolds me and pleasures me in surprising ways

A I receive a loving note/text/email for no special reason from my loved one.

E my partner and I grow other intimacies during the day

B I get to spend uninterrupted quality time with my partner.

C my partner and I spontaneously have sex in a new/different location

A I receive sexy texts/messages about what my partner is going to do to me later.

C my partner gives me something sexy that shows he/she was thinking of me.

E I sit close to my partner, feel our intimate connection.

A I am genuinely complimented and told how desirable I am to him/her.

B my partner takes the time to learn about my body.

D my partner does exactly what I had been asking for in bed.

B we bond in a couple's retreat or workshop.

C my partner and I play sex games before playing with one another

A my partner reacts positively to something I've done to them sensually/sexually.

D my partner follows my directions in the bedroom, even if they usually do not.

E my partner and I kiss frequently.

B I sense my partner is showing more interest in my oral pleasure.

D my partner unexpectedly does something for me, like running a bath.

E my partner and I touch, lock eyes and breathe together.

E my partner puts his/her arm around me and pulls me close.

C my partner surprises me with a gift that makes me feel desired.

B I have a long, sensual session with my partner.

A I hear sexy, supportive words while we are pleasuring each other.

B we have hectic lives, but he/she schedules time with me.

E we hold each other and I feel our connection.

A I'm complimented by my partner, letting me know I still turn him/her on.

B my partner takes the time to listen to what I really desire in the bedroom.

E my partner and I share non-sexual contact that leads to a sexual encounter.

D my partner offers to do that thing I said I wanted.

D my partner creates one of my fantasies.

C my partner and I play fight or tickle which leads to sexual encounter

E my partner and I breathe together and connect

A I hear my partner say how good I feel to them

D my partner doesn't ask questions, but does exactly what I ask.

B my partner asks about and accepts my sexual desires.

C my partner brings me a gift to increase / improve my climax.

D My partner and I explore a kink we've discussed

A I hear "I want you" from my partner.

C my partner buys something to enhance intimate play for me.

A I hear my partner's moans during intimate sessions

B I'm stressed so my partner rubs my feet/back and gives orgasm to release tension.

C my partner brings me something that I have been wanting for awhile

D my partner does tasks for my pleasure.

E my partner and I have an intimate tantric session connecting on a different level

B my partner touches/licks me all over.

A my partner says how good I am and/or feel during intimate sessions.

C my partner gives me toys/lube/lotions to enhance our intimate play.

D we try bondage, me tying him/her up or him/her tying me up.

E we turn off the lights, eyes closed, quiet, energy exchange sexual session.

B my partner gives me oral satisfaction until climax.

C my partner gives me an expensive gift.

D being spanked/choked by my partner or vice versa.

A sending messages / pictures to my partner that he/she tells you excites them.

E feeling me and my partner reach climax together.

C my partner buys chocolate, honey, whipped cream, etc to use on each other.

How many of each letter did you receive?

A: _____

B: _____

C:_____

D:_____

E:_____

Did you (or your partner) receive mostly …

A's? The Conversationalist – You/They enjoy hearing the words. You/They want you to tell them you love, appreciate, adore them. Try sending your Conversationalist a sweet, but sexy text in the middle of the day. Tell them what you are going to do, then do it. It also turns them on to hear your voice / moans during love making sessions. Dirty Talk is such a beautiful skill to learn!

B's? The Seductive – You/They love long, sensual intimate sessions. Pay particular attention to pleasing Seductives orally. Reserve an entire evening for your interaction, increased intensity kissing mingled with conversations about what turns them on. Try giving a full body massage with either edible or pheromone infused oil. This type also needs a shorter To-Do List to completely enjoy themselves.

C's? The Creator – You/They love to be playful or engage in costume play. You/They enjoy adding

131

people, places or things to their sexual play. You show Creators how much you care by picking up aphrodisiacs, jewelry or lingerie on the way home or that incredible toy that will help achieve a mind -blowing orgasm! Try taking a trip for a change in scenery.

D's? The Sweetest Taboo – You/They enjoy the push and pull in the bedroom. Many Sweet Taboos have a dominant personality in the bedroom or can be a switch. You/They are excited by shaking things up, role playing or adding toys. To please, try BDSM activities, bondage tape, paddles, under the bed restraints or becoming the Dom(me) or submissive for the evening. Try the Power Play workshop for some tips on how to play in a style that will appeal to you both. Sweet Taboos are also turned on by you doing tasks outside of the bedroom to get them in the mood.

E's? Rainbow Children – You/They enjoy the transcendence of the sexual act. You/They want to feel the spiritual connection. Rainbow Children enjoy long kissing sessions and intense sensations. Try attending a tantric sex workshop. Learn how to breathe together. Take my Couple's Bonding Workshop. Turn off the lights and allow them to simply enjoy you.

All about even? Changelings! You/They like everything! (Depending on their mood) This is the type that cannot be bored. They want to explore various kinks, may have a fetish or two and have no problems with toys or new situations. Their bucket list is always being updated. They also have a curiosity about most things, especially what excites you, so try taking a few classes together.

Wishing you amazing days and steamy nights of Sexual Intimacy!

This is your moment! Your

- radioactive spider bite

- vat of acid submersion

- gamma radiation exposure

- super saiyan transformation

- alien artifact discovery

- rebirth as a mutant **moment!**

With your newfound knowledge and a little practice …

You will become Unstoppable!

About The Author

Jai Simone, author, keynote speaker, poet, educator, activist, Domme, anime and comic fan, world traveler, shoe lover, partner, and mom, ... has been seen on countless stages, from New York to Honolulu, Toronto to Mexico City, Seattle to London. She has blazed stages and changed lives. Also a media darling, she has been featured on television, in print, online and hosting The Intimacy Superpower Podcast and co-hosting The Walking Desires podcast.

Jai Simone is also the founder and CEO of Catalyst Life Global and a certified life and intimacy coach who is best known for guiding individuals and couples to stand in their power using tailored approaches and private talk sessions. Through these steps, clients are able to take action, discover the beauty and magic in themselves, and get the life and outcomes they desire.

Catalyst Life Global is a wellness, education, and relationship success company. From speaking engagements to empowerment events to single's, couple's and corporate retreats, we help people rediscover the intimate connections and pleasure in their lives. Cat-Life specializes in assisting you become the happiest, most productive, successful and fulfilled version of yourself. Let's discover your superpowers!

www.jaisimone.com

www.theintimacysuperpower.com

www.catalystlifeglobal.com

www.ingramcontent.com/pod-product-compliance
Lightning Source LLC
Chambersburg PA
CBHW070252290326
41930CB00041B/2459

9 780979 619809